TRANSFORMATION WOMAN II WOMAN PRAYER JOURNAL

DR. SHAUNTAE WARREN

It is our prayer and declaration that you would maintain a Spirit of Integrity concerning the knowledge shared with you in this book. Meaning when using the information in this book publicly, you would give the author, Dr. Shauntae Warren proper recognition and acknowledgement for the knowledge, work, experience, research, and labor of development for this book.

No part of this book may be reproduced by copying or any other method of duplication unless expressed written permission has been granted by Dr. Shauntae Warren.

Thank You In Advance
for you countenance of righteousness and obedience.

Ecclesiastes 12:14

For God shall bring every work into judgment, with every secret thing, whether it be good or whether it be evil.

First Edition: 2021

ISBN: 978-1-934905-97-5

Worldwide Kingdom Publishing
1911 Horger St
Lincoln Park, Michigan 48146

Copyright 2021 by DR. SHAUNTAE WARREN
All rights reserved.

DEDICATION

As I sit and think about who to dedicate this book to, so many thoughts and people cross my mind.

I must say, I dedicate this book to my grandmother Rosetta McDowell. She was a woman I watched fight and persevere for her family. As she prayed and watched, there was a special grace. The grace of a wife, mother, friend, and a prayer warrior for many, who may never knew she ever prayed for them. I watched her transition in a very unique way as she battled through Alzheimer's. She still maintained her fight all the way until her promotion with the Lord. A true champion who fought for me and passed that mantle onto my mom. My mom continued to fight for me and her family. They were both examples of what being a strong woman looked like. They faced many obstacles yes, they stood with God's grace and strength. I love them both and thank them for being examples of a Champion.

SPECIAL THANKS

To my Hubby, Wes Warren, I love you. Thank you for pushing me past my own limitations.

My children, The Fab Five, I appreciate your support and how you have allowed me to freely be shared with others.

To my spiritual mom, Dr. Charisse Lewis, thanks for helping me birth the vision.

To the Nation of Elohim, my EKM family, I love you all so much and thank you for believing in God's vision for me.

To W2W, you women soar, and you are the reason why I never can give up. You keep me reaching higher.

To Genesis, thank you for our long summer and your patience working with me in writing this journal.

FOREWARD

It is with great elation that I sit to write this foreward for this much needed journal. I am Dr. Sabrina Jackson and I have written several books, I am a clinical therapist, evangelist, and radio.tv personality. However, the role that lead me to meet Dr. Warren is that of Professional Speaker. Many years ago, I was doing a series of workshops for Headstart specifically for couples. Well, Shauntae was instrumental with making sure I was selected to be a speaker. I later learned that she was inspired to speak and train after witnessing me as a Black woman move in such confidence. Now, let me be clear, I am confident however it is because I know God is using me.

Now, let's fast forward many years, I run into this powerhouse as the leader of a church and was asked to speak. She shared her testimony of how she fasted many life challenges. I know that this vessel is anointed to speak to the hearts of those struggling with depression, trauma, and lack of feeling worthy. Dr. Warren has put together a masterpiece with activities, guided questions, and prayers all designed to help you discover the you GOD sees!!. This is such a great tool to aid in self care as it is a requirement not just a recommendation.

I am excited for you as you commit to yourself and embark on TRANSFORMATION!! There is often a misconception about transformation that it is all sweet and pretty. NOT SO, the butterfly is first a creepy crawly thing, however once that cocoon incubation occurs….a unique beautiful butterfly emerges. YOU are on your way to being that Butterfly being carefully and lovingly guided there by Dr. Shauntae Warren, a woman who has not allowed her past to determine her future. She is a wife, mother, minister, talk show host, University founder, and so much more.

Dr. Sabrina "The People Expert"
Peace Ambassador to the UN
Clinical Therapist, Evangelist, Author
Creator of Essential Colors, Essential Lovestyles, and the Essential YOU Collection
www.sabrinajackson.com

FOREWARD

I am so excited for you, Dr. Shauntae Warren, you are an extraordinary Woman of God, a woman of God's agape love. I have watched you grow and mature into an anointed remarkable Woman of God. You are a devoted Wife, loving Mother, dedicated Pastor, accurate Prophetess, Psalmist who worships with abandonment, listening Counselor, clear Teacher, strong Mentor, patient Spiritual Mother, neutral Relationship Navigator, Kingdom Business-Woman, Co-Owner of Elohim Kingdom University, Prophetic Recording Artist, and a New Author. Everything God has for you is manifesting in this season! I am so elated as your Spiritual Mother and Apostle to witness and partake in the birth of such an Awesome move of God flowing through you. Truly, the scripture tells us according I Corinthians 2:9, *But as it is written, Eye hath not seen, nor ear heard, neither have entered into the heart of man, the things which God hath prepared for them that love him.*

Truly, there is more within the depths of your Spirit (your inner man) that God is going to birth through you. There shall be many more books, journals, worship and teaching cd's, and new creative ideas to mature women in their spiritual walk with God. You shall ascend into new realms of power in the realm of the Spirit and the Lord shall share His intricate secrets with you. It is through the power of the prophetic that the lives of people shall be changed. Many shall come out of darkness and enter into His marvelous light!

TRANSFORMATION JOURNAL shall change the minds of those who have been experiencing defeat, discouragement, depression, brokenness and many other obstacles that have interfere with the progress of others. This journal is an interactive self-help book to walk people out of bondage. Through prayer, scripture, and experience Dr. Shauntae Warren shows every reader how to experience breakthrough by changing the mindset from being a victim to becoming victorious believer! You will forever be transformed once you read and complete the assignments in Transformation Journal "The Mind of A Champion"!!!!

Dr. Shauntae Warren, God is pleased with your humility and honesty! Keep up the excellent work of the Kingdom!!!

Dr. Charissee Lewis, Apostle
Overseer of Worldwide Kingdom Network of Churches
Creator Developing Healthy Eating
Host of Kingdom Vision, Hour of Power, & Destined for Greatness Shows
Accredited Liquid Fire Training Center
CEO of Starr Cosmetics
Ecclesiastical Leadership Teacher
Love Doctor of Love On Fire
Worldwide Kingdom Publishing
Author & Counselor
www.drcharisseelewis.com

TABLE OF CONTENTS

Week One	Recognition		
Sunday	Recognizing A Time For Change	page	15
Monday	Recognizing Distractions	page	19
Tuesday	Recognizing Rejection	page	22
Wednesday	Recognizing Rebellion & The Action of Disobedience	page	25
Thursday	Recognizing Fear	page	28
Friday	Recognizing Anger	page	32
Saturday	Recognizing Guilt and Shame	page	36

Week Two	Acceptance/Forgiveness		
Sunday	Forgiveness of Self	page	40
Monday	Childhood Pain & Parents	page	44
Tuesday	Forgiveness of Family	page	48
Wednesday	Friends, Associates, & Co-Workers	page	52
Thursday	Forgiveness of Failed Relationships	page	56
Friday	Forgiveness of Those in Authority	page	60
Saturday	Acceptance: Time To Move Forward	page	65

Week Three	Identification of Now		
Sunday	Do You Know Who You Are?	page	70
Monday	Why Choosing You is Important?	page	75
Tuesday	Do You Have a Blueprint?	page	81
Wednesday	Operational Plan	page	85
Thursday	The Power of the Atmosphere that You Carry	page	91
Friday	Beauty From the Inside Out	page	95
Saturday	Staying Heart Happy	page	100

Week Four	Fulfillment The Mindset of Champion		
Sunday	What Are You Thinking	page	104
Monday	What's In Your Soil?	page	109
Tuesday	An Interview with My Thoughts	page	113
Wednesday	Identifying Emotional Distress	page	117
Thursday	The Power of Focus	page	122
Friday	Pushing Forward	page	127
Saturday	The Mindset of A Champion	page	132

Week 1: Recognition

Sunday
Recognizing a Time For Change

If we confess our sins, He is faithful and righteous to forgive us our sins and cleanse us from all unrighteousness- 1 John 1:9

It is time to recognize there is a need for change. Are you sick and tired of revolving cycles of restraint and opposition in your life? On today, I want you to think of anything in your life that causes you to feel pain, fear, depressed, defeated, or anxiety.

Write them down here:

_____
_____
_____
_____
_____
_____
_____
_____
_____
_____
_____
_____
_____

Week 1: Recognition

Exercise:

Sit for 8 minutes to quiet your thoughts. Relax your mind.

_____
_____
_____
_____
_____
_____
_____
_____

Prayer:

Father in the Name of Jesus, I thank You for my life. Thank You for my mind. I ask that You would touch my thoughts on today, and cause any thoughts that are impure to be eradicated from my thought realm. I ask that You would remove bad memories from my mind, and subconscious. Thank You for removing the spirit of hurt and pain out of my life. Even negative thoughts that cycle in my mind and that are displayed in my emotions; I ask You, Father God, to heal them now. God, I am asking You to reveal any thoughts lying dormant, that would try to stop me from receiving change in my life. I thank You, Lord, in Jesus' Name. Amen.

Week 1: Recognition

Write the Thoughts of God:

Week 1: Recognition
Write the Thoughts of God:

Week 1: Recognition

Monday
Recognizing Distractions

"Look straight ahead and fix your eyes on what lies before you." Proverbs 4:25

Do you find yourself dealing with distractions which cause you to detour from the set plan or course that was once designed for you to succeed? Distractions are designed to get you off track, which causes the mindset of defeat. Today, you need to write down all the people, places, or things in your life that are distractions.

Write them down here:

People:_____
_____
_____
_____

Places:_____
_____
_____
_____

Things:_____
_____
_____
_____

Week 1: Recognition

Exercise:

Starting today, set three goals for the week to start the process of completing the assignment(s) God has given you. Completing these goals, will bring a sense of achievement and ultimately destroy the feeling of defeat in your mind.

1)_____

_____

2)_____

_____

3)_____

_____

Prayer:

Lord, I thank You for giving me the strength to remove distractions of all kinds, out of my life. Lord, I submit my will to You. On today, I ask You to lead me, guide me, and instruct me in Godly wisdom and counsel concerning my life. God, I thank You for delivering me from any works of the flesh that may be operating in my life. Lord, deliver me from people, places, and things that may cause me to be distracted from Your divine purpose and plan that you have ordained for me in Jesus' Name, I pray. Amen.

Week 1: Recognition
Write the Thoughts of God:

Week 1: Recognition

Tuesday
Recognizing Rejection

For ye have not received the spirit of bondage again to fear, but ye have received the Spirit of adoption, whereby we cry, "Abba! Father!"-Romans 8:15

Do you often find yourself with feelings of loneliness? Do you feel like you don't fit in? Do you have feelings of being misunderstood, or unaccepted? If you do, there is a great possibility that you are dealing with the spirit of rejection. In many cases, when looking at our first introduction to relationships which would be paternal; they have an influential part in who we become. If we have not been properly insulated or validated in who God has created us to be, then when we are rejected, the seed of rejection is more susceptible to you.

Exercise:

On today, identify areas in your life where you may have been rejected and it continues to play in your mind.

_____
_____
_____
_____
_____
_____
_____
_____
_____
_____

Week 1: Recognition

Prayer:

Father in the Name of Jesus, I thank You for showing me areas where the seed of rejection has been planted in me. God, I ask You to break negative thoughts and negative interpretations from out of my heart. God, I thank You for freeing me today from everything that You revealed to me, and eradicating rejection out of my memory. God, I thank You for freeing me from thoughts and pain from past actions. I thank You for guarding my heart. I thank You for setting me free and healing me from where the spirit of rejection has been in my life. In Jesus Name, I pray. Amen.

Write the Thoughts of God:

_____
_____
_____
_____
_____
_____
_____
_____
_____
_____
_____

Week 1: Recognition

Write the Thoughts of God

Week 1: Recognition

Wednesday
Recognizing Rebellion & the Action of Disobedience

"Why do you call me 'Lord, Lord,' and not do what I tell you?"-Luke 6:46

Oftentimes, when we rebel against the things that we are supposed to do, we don't understand that it is an act of disobedience. Essentially, it opens the door for stagnation in our lives. We must get into divine alignment in the things that God is calling for us to do. For example: Maybe you know God is requiring you to go deeper in your relationship with Him. However, you are rebelling due to the spirit of fear; because you are afraid of change. You may fear the responsibility, or fear what others may say or think. You may even fear having to give up worldly habits. Ultimately, causing you to disobey by not reading your bible, not going to church, or not answering the call of God on your life, in its entirety. Write down areas where you walk in disobedience and after, look at the root of why you disobey and rebel.

1. _____
2. _____
3. _____
4. _____
5. _____

What is the root of disobedience?

_____
_____

Week 1: Recognition

Exercise

Pick an area in your life where you disobey. For the next 30 days walk in obedience by choosing to make the right decision. What are you going to do when disobedience comes before you? Choose and write below:

_____
_____
_____
_____
_____

Prayer

Father, I come to you humbly in my heart. I am asking that You would show me the areas of rebellion and disobedience that are in my life. I ask You to remove them out of my heart. I know that when I walk in disobedience it is not pleasing to You. I choose to live in obedience and I will no longer rebel against Your word. I choose to submit to You Father in every area of my life. God, I ask You to heal my heart from anyone who has hurt me, violated me, or any situation that has brought me pain. I ask God that You would go into the crevices of my heart and that You would fill it with Your agape love. I am asking You to order my steps and bind my feet to Your will and Your way. I ask You to bring peace to my mind and my thoughts. I thank You, Father, I will not operate in the soulish realm of thinking; but I will be obedient to follow Your word and Your call for me to live and to love. In Jesus' name, Amen.

Week 1: Recognition

Write the Thoughts of God:

Week 1: Recognition

Thursday

Recognizing Fear

"For God has not given us a spirit of fear, but of power and of love and of a sound mind"- 2 Timothy 1:7

We know that fear is the opposite of faith. Without faith, it is impossible to please God and because of this reason, we cannot operate in fear. It is the ultimate plan of the enemy to have us be fearful of launching forward in faith. He tries to bombard our thoughts with doubt, fear, unbelief, and skepticism which refrain us from being able to move in the unseen realm of what God has promised us. Oftentimes, this stagnates us from receiving all that God has for us or has called for us to do.

Exercise:

Write down eight scriptures that deal with faith and begin to read them before you start your day. Write down anything or anyone that generates fear. After you write down your fears, make a declaration to renounce fear from each of the fears you wrote down.

1) _____ 2) _____

3) _____ 4) _____

5) _____ 6) _____

7) _____ 8) _____

Week 1: Recognition

Fears: _____

_____

_____

_____

_____

Declarations: _____

_____

_____

_____

_____

Example: If I fear to launch my new business because I have failed at things in the past. I would say: "Lord, I thank you for delivering me from the fear of failure."

Week 1: Recognition

Prayer:
God, I repent from operating in the spirit of fear. God, I thank You for making my faith whole. I thank You, God, for removing fear from my life. For I know fear draws the enemy, and it is not of You. God, I thank You that I will begin to trust You with my whole heart. I will trust You in the hard places in my life. God, I thank You, that You have given me power, unconditional love, and You ministered peace to my emotions. God, I thank You that in times of uncertainty that I will turn to You and I will not fear the world's consequences. Lord, I shall trust in You with my whole heart and I will acknowledge You. By doing so, I know that You shall direct my path. Father, You said that You would give me perfect peace; if I operate in the mind of Christ. I thank You today, that I have no more fear in Jesus' Name, Amen.

Week 1: Recognition

Write the Thoughts of God:

_____
_____
_____
_____
_____
_____
_____

Week 1: Recognition

Write the Thoughts of God:

Week 1: Recognition

Friday

Recognizing Anger

"My dear brothers and sisters, take note of this: Everyone should be quick to listen, slow to speak and slow to become angry because human anger does not produce the righteousness that God desires."- James 1:19-20

Anger is a destructive emotion that clouds us from good judgment. Anger is a natural emotion but when it is not properly managed; it can become cancer to the heart and the body. It opens the door to maliciousness, strife, revenge, rage, wrath, arguing, fighting, spite, unforgiveness, sickness, and more. If you find yourself being used by the spirit of anger, ultimately, you are holding yourself captive from receiving true happiness and the agape love from the Father. When we operate in the manifestation of anger, outwardly, or inwardly, it can be hazardous to the atmosphere that we create or to the people we love. We must learn how to communicate when we feel like we have been hurt or wronged; and not allow these emotions to fester on the inside of us. We must be mindful to not use our tongue as a weapon of evil; instead, we should use our tongue as a weapon of truth and love. It is important as well, that we do not use our physical bodies to bring forth hurt or harm. It is time to begin to gain control over unrighteous anger and move into the peace of God in all situations.

Exercise:

Identify when your anger is elevating and take a Selah, a break. If you had a stressful day, find time to listen to a CD, or do a calming exercise.

Week 1: Recognition

Example: You can do this exercise in the car on the way to work or coming from work. Or even on the way to pick up the children from school.

Take the time to write down certain situations or people that trigger your anger. Then think of ways to react in peace or avoid the situations, or even gain a new perspective or outlook.

_____
_____
_____
_____
_____
_____
_____
_____
_____
_____
_____
_____
_____
_____
_____
_____
_____
_____
_____

Week 1: Recognition

Prayer:

Master and Savior, I come to You in repentance where I have moved out of my anger. I ask that You remove evil out of my heart. God, I ask that You would arrest any emotions that cause this spirit to operate in my life. Father, You said, that if I think about things that are true, that are honorable, that are right, that are pure, that are lovely, of a good report and things that are worthy of praise; I believe it will help the spirit of peace to reside in my life. When situations arise that try to provoke anger, I will make a conscious decision to walk in peace and love, in Jesus' Name, Amen.

Write the Thoughts of God:

_____
_____
_____
_____
_____
_____
_____
_____
_____
_____
_____

Week 1: Recognition

Write the Thoughts of God:
(Con't)

Week 1: Recognition

Saturday
Recognizing Guilt and Shame

"For God did not send His Son into the world to condemn the world; but that the world through Him might be saved." John 3:17

As you sit on day 7 of this journal, my prayer is that you feel a new liberty; because of the healing and deliverance that has begun to take place in your life. On this day, we will look at guilt and shame. Many times we hold ourselves captive from past decisions that we have made, that may have been out of alignment for God's will for our lives. Or maybe even violations that have taken place, that cause us to walk in shame. Sometimes we take on the guilt of things that have happened in our lives that were completely out of our control. Today, you need to release all guilt and drop all of the charges against yourself. Do not allow Satan to harbor unhealthy thoughts, emotions, or outlooks on who God has called for you to be. You are fearfully and wonderfully made, created in the image of God in His pure likeness. It is time to recognize and identify who you are by not allowing guilt or shame to hold you bound for another moment.

Exercise

Look in the mirror and begin to say "I release myself from guilt and shame because I am _____." Start to decree positive affirmations over yourself for the next 7 days.

Week 1: Recognition

Affirmations

1) _____

2) _____

3) _____

4) _____

5) _____

6) _____

7) _____

Prayer

God, I thank You for releasing me from guilt and shame, from feelings that would make me want to hide. I release myself from not feeling worthy to receive all that You have for me. Lord, I thank You that I will no longer walk in condemnation or blame myself for any decisions I have made that weren't Your will for my life. I thank You, God, that the enemy can no longer torment me because who the Son sets free is free indeed. Father, thank You for causing the light of Your countenance to shine upon me. I am content in You and who You have called for me to be. I thank You for my past teaching me how to move forward with lessons of wisdom. I thank You for the skin I am in and I thank You that I am free to be me.

Week 1: Recognition

Write the Thoughts of God:

Week 1: Recognition

Write the Thoughts of God:
(Con't)

Week 2: Forgiveness/Acceptance

Sunday
Forgiveness of Self

(Bad choices, mistakes, violations, lack of trust)

"Therefore, if anyone is in Christ, he is a new creation. The old has passed away; behold, the new has come."- 2 Corinthians 5:17-18

On today, you have to look at the power of forgiving yourself. Often times, the enemy likes to hold us to our past failures. When we reflect on past mistakes in our lives or bad decisions, it can cause us to harbor unforgiveness in our hearts towards ourselves (for making decisions) and others. When we harbor unforgiveness toward ourselves, it holds us in bondage to our past failures; and it hinders us from moving forward in our God-given purpose. Sometimes, it may seems that we have moved forward in the natural but our spirit man is still stagnant. We need to move forward in spiritual freedom to grow. We also have to look at how these decisions may affect our trust in God and others. If violations occurred in your life, it opens up feelings of self-blame, unworthiness, guilt, and shame. We have to learn not to be a prisoner of things that are in our control or out of our control that have caused trauma or pain in our lives. A way to set ourselves free is through forgiveness. We can no longer operate in self-hatred because it is a sin. At this moment, choose to forgive yourself set yourself free through the power of forgiveness in Jesus' Mighty Name.

Week 2: Forgiveness/Acceptance

Exercise

Get in a quiet place, relax your thoughts, and ask God to show you if you harbor any un-forgiveness towards yourself because of a bad decision that you made. Ask God if you are harboring un-forgiveness if there were natural violations that have taken place in your life. Next, write them down and go through your list and begin to declare that you choose to forgive that person, and/or yourself. If there are situations that are holding you to the spirit of un-forgiveness, declare that you will release yourself from the pain, the hurt, or disappointment that came through the decisions that were made. Finally, declare II Corinthians 5:17-18 and John 8:36 over your life.

Prayer:

Father in the Name of Jesus, I thank You for showing me these areas of un-forgiveness in my heart. God, I ask that today, You would set me free from the spirit of un-forgiveness of self. God, I ask that You would remove past hurts, and past failures. God, I ask You to deliver me: even where there were violations in my life where I may have been taken advantage of, God heal me. I ask that You would cleanse my heart and cleanse my mind. God, I ask that You would wash my thoughts, cleanse my emotions, my imagination, and my memory of these situations. Lord, help me to make a decision today to forgive myself and anyone who has wronged me. I choose today to not allow un-forgiveness to hold me captive. God, I choose freedom on today, and Father, I thank You that He who the Son sets free, is free indeed, according to John 8:36 in Jesus Name, Amen.

Week 2: Forgiveness/Acceptance

Write the Thoughts of God:

Week 2: Forgiveness/Acceptance

Write the Thoughts of God:
(Con't)

Week 2: Forgiveness/Acceptance

Monday
Childhood Pain & Parents

"For I know the plans I have for you," declares the Lord, "plans to prosper you and not harm you, plans to give you hope and a future."-Jeremiah 29:11

When we think of our childhood, we think of it as a time in our lives that should be remembered as joyous and shaping us for our future. Unfortunately, there are times when parents miss the mark due to what they have experienced growing up. Even current life situations can interfere with their parenting skills. However, we have to make a conscious decision to forgive them. When we hold un-forgiveness in our in our hearts, it hinders our prayers, our relationships, and the beauty of rebuilding healthy relationships with our parents. No longer can we allow the enemy to replay in our thoughts bad experiences; we had to endure as we grew up. You must choose to give this portion of your life to God and allow Him to bring forth inner healing. If your parents are deceased, healing can still take place through the power of forgiveness and receiving the love of the Father.

Exercise:

On today write a letter to your parent(s) whether they are here or made their transition. In this letter, express all of your emotions and the memories that hold you captive. The purpose of this exercise is to bring forth freedom in your thoughts and start cleansing your mind from hurt and pain that may have been caused when you were a child. In addition, I would suggest that you seek out help from your spiritual leader or counselor to continue navigating you through a process of healing.

Week 2: Forgiveness/Acceptance

At the proper time, you may choose to share what you wrote but the purpose and intent is to begin the healing process in your heart.

Prayer:

God, I ask that today You would heal my heart from any pain that was caused in my childhood. God, I ask that You would bring up things that have been buried that happened to me that I have not healed from. God, I ask that You would eradicate them through the fire of the Holy Spirit. Lord, I ask that would remove bad memories that try to haunt my thoughts. Even where there may have been a disappointment, where my parents did not do the things that they should have done as parents. God, I ask that You would even forgive them. God, I surrender my will unto You today. God, I trust You with my life and my future. God, I thank You for releasing new joy and new strength. God, I thank You starting today that forgiveness is a choice for me. I choose to forgive my parents or anyone who has caused me to hurt, pain, or fear as a child. God, I thank You for giving me new strength and a new strategy to move forward in my life. No longer will the baggage from my childhood hinder me in moving forward in my adulthood or even with my children. Father, I thank You that this will not be transferred to the people who I love and care about. I thank You for Your healing power in Jesus' Name.

Exercise:

Now that you forgiven, say out loud, *"I DROP THE CHARGES!"*

Week 2: Forgiveness/Acceptance

Write the Thoughts of God:

Week 2: Forgiveness/Acceptance

Write the Thoughts of God:
(Con't)

Week 2: Forgiveness/Acceptance

Tuesday
Forgiveness of Family

Bear with each other and forgive one another if any of you has a grievance against someone. Forgive as the Lord forgave you- Colossians 3:13

The family unit is a powerful entity. Time after time, we find a family in dysfunction through lack of communication, misunderstanding, jealousy, sibling rivalry, addictions, and the list goes on. We must learn how to communicate with our family members when we feel offended or misunderstandings happen. When we abort healthy communication of our true feelings, it could begin a pathway for un-forgiveness to set up in our hearts. No longer can we talk to others in the family or other siblings about the family member who we felt wronged us. When we do this, it opens up the spiritual doors for the seed of discord, division in the family, and negativity. We truly must hold fast to the family being ordained by God. We truly must hold fast to the family and obey it. As we walk in forgiveness, we will begin to see the power of unity rise in our family structures, and satan will be defeated throughout every generation of our families.

Exercise

Pray for family or siblings for 30 days. Pray positive prayers, not condemning prayers. Pray loving prayers that will encourage unity and oneness in the family. Prayers that will strengthen the family bond and cause families to work, play, and pray together.

Week 2: Forgiveness/Acceptance

Prayer

Lord, I thank You for the power of forgiveness. God, I ask that You would forgive me for holding onto any hurt or pain that has been caused by my siblings or relatives. Lord, strengthen my communication and give me holy boldness to be able to communicate how I feel in times of disagreement. I ask that today, that the enemy will not use me to gossip or slander those who I love. God, even if there have been times where I was a victim of slander or character assassination; I choose to forgive those in my family. Lord, I thank You that You would use me to shine the unconditional love of God throughout my family. I thank You for giving me a new standard of what Your agape love means. Father, I thank You that I will begin to pray for my family and decree and declare blessings and not curses over my family. God, I thank You for covering my family and bringing new unity and new order in my family structure. In Jesus' Name, Amen.

Exercise:

Write a short prayer on unity that you can pray for your family.

_____
_____
_____
_____
_____
_____
_____

Week 2: Forgiveness/Acceptance

Write the Thoughts of God:

Week 2: Forgiveness/Acceptance

Write the Thoughts of God:
(Con't)

Week 2: Forgiveness/Acceptance

Wednesday
Friends, Associates, & Co-workers

"And be ye kind one to another, tenderhearted, forgiving one another, even as God for Christ's sake hath forgiven you."-Ephesians 4:32

Commonly, we may work with people who have falsely accused us on the job. Friendships or associates who may have backstabbed us. Contrary to how we have been wronged, we have to be open to receiving what forgiveness brings to us. If we don't, it gives the person power over us. It can be frustrating; but we have to remember harboring unforgiveness holds us in bondage. Their emotions are controlling our actions. If we don't forgive, it keeps us stifled and effects the environment in which, we work. It can cause stress, hostility, discord, and stifle the team from accomplishing goals. What is the payoff if you decide not to forgive? Let me tell you, it is torture to you. Many times, we hold onto negativity subconsciously. It can consume us, and what is in your head will begin to manifest in our attitudes and truly motivate us. It is time to forgive them for they don't know what they do. Do not get caught up in that merry go round of thinking why the person may have lied, and slandered you, etc. Because most times, the person doesn't even know why they may have done negative actions against you. Instead, begin to realize backbiting, lies, misunderstandings, and betrayal, all come to help kill the flesh to get to your next dimension of love. This is what it means to have the ability to love your enemies and truly have love as the standard. Be open to forgiveness that way others emotions won't dictate your actions and mess with the way God has ordained you to love.

Week 2: Forgiveness/Acceptance

Exercise:

Be able to identify if you're holding an un-forgiveness.

1. Ask God if you need to communicate.

   _____

2. If you do communicate, you have to accept the person may not have a proper answer or understanding response. Can you handle that?

   _____

3. Are you able to recognize the evaluation in forgiveness?

   _____

Prayer

Father in the Name of Jesus, God, I thank You for the ability to receive Your forgiveness. God, search my heart today and go into those places where people have talked against me, lied on me, or where I have done this to someone else. God, show me where I can do better next time. I choose to drop the charges today and move forward. Lord, release those strongholds out of my heart. God, I thank You that in atmospheres and environments where I would feel a yoke, it would be destroyed. God, You said in Your word that Your yoke is easy and Your burden is light. God, I thank You for strengthening my heart and my understanding. I thank You that my emotions are in divine alignment with Your will for my life. God, give me the ability to love my enemies and the power to forgive. I will give You all the praise, honor and glory In Jesus' Name, Amen.

Week 2: Forgiveness/Acceptance

Write the Thoughts of God:

Week 2: Forgiveness/Acceptance

Write the Thoughts of God:
(Con't)

Week 2: Forgiveness/Acceptance

Thursday
Forgiveness of Failed Relationships

"Let all bitterness, and wrath, and anger, and clamor, and evil speaking, be put away from you, with all malice: And be ye kind one to another, tenderhearted, forgiving one another, even as God for Christ's sake hath forgiven you."-Ephesians 4:31-32

After a failed relationship, we must walk in forgiveness, no matter what happened in the relationship. We should look at the relationship through a positive lens. Not as a state of failure, but as a lesson learned. When looking at it as a lesson learned, we must forgive ourselves and let go of feelings of uncertainties. We start thinking what we could have done differently to work out the relationship and trying to understand why we got into the relationship from the beginning. Or feelings of disappointment, grief, guilt, revenge, and rebellion. Forgiveness is a choice, an action that requires one to evaluate themselves, as well as the situation while releasing the other party from any wrongs they may have done. Walking in forgiveness is a deliberate action, it may not be easy but it is necessary so that you can walk in freedom and receive what God has for you in your present and your future. Un-forgiveness blocks the true power of God's love from being able to penetrate our hearts. To move forward in another marriage or relationship healthy and successfully, you have to operate in the power of forgiveness.

Exercise:

Take the next five days and write a love letter to yourself. Tell yourself why you are enough and valuable and why someone would be blessed to be in a relationship with you.

Week 2: Forgiveness/Acceptance

Work willingly at whatever you do, as though you were working for the Lord rather than for people.- Colossians 3:23

Prayer:
Father in the Name of Jesus, I thank You that You are setting me free from the spirit of unforgiveness in any failed relationship. I choose to forgive_____ (the person/people who wronged you) for_____ (what they did wrong). I ask that You would go into the corridors and crevices of my heart, and that You would bring divine healing. I ask that You would allow blood to flow and pump through the areas of my heart that have hardened. The places in my heart where I have placed walls around, and bob wire is surrounding my heart. Lord, I ask that You would tear it down. Lord, I ask that You would and teach me how to love with Your agape love, and how to function in a healthy relationship. God, I ask that You would shield and cover my heart; because You said out of my heart flows the issues of life. God, I ask that You would teach me how to trust without fear. God, I ask that You would show me how to understand even as people disappoint me. God, I pray that the spirit of unforgiveness would not reattach itself to me ever again. I thank You that the joy of the Lord is my strength. God, I stand in expectancy in believing You for every promise You have promised me. Father, You said in Isaiah 61:3, that You would release unto me *"the oil of joy for mourning and the garment of praise for the spirit of heaviness."* Lord, I receive the new oil and a new mantle of joy today! I thank You that I am walking in new freedom. I thank You that I am free to love again, to live again, and to laugh again! In Jesus' Name.

Week 2: Forgiveness/Acceptance

Write the Thoughts of God:

Week 2: Forgiveness/Acceptance

Write the Thoughts of God:
(Con't)

Week 2: Forgiveness/Acceptance

Friday
Forgiveness of Those in Authority

(spiritual leader, teachers, bosses, coaches, mentors, etc)

"For if you forgive other people when they sin against you, your heavenly Father will also forgive you. But if you do not forgive others their sins, your Father will not forgive your sins."-Matthew 6:14-15

Part A: It is necessary to release the spirit of hurt and pain. Many of us have submitted to those who are in authority over us. We have allowed our hearts to be open and we have been vulnerable with these people in our lives. When these relationships are severed, it can cause deep hurt or trauma because we were open to those we served or worked for. If you are looking in the area of work relationships or coaches, supervisors it can be detrimental because that is your place of work. You may have experienced verbal abuse, been overlooked, or belittled, this can cause stress, anger, anxiety, and feelings of overwhelmed-ness and depression. We have to learn how to communicate effectively and operate in the spirit of holy boldness. Also, understand we are not the "boss" but we still have rights and values. If you are dealing with the fear of authority, you must be set free so you can operate in the workplace, on your team, etc.

Part B: When you are dealing with hurt from spiritual leaders or mentors this can cause trauma because we look at these people as a safe place. When there is verbal or physiological abuse, emotional manipulation, or control present, it cuts deep. We have to learn how to be loyal to God first and when we notice red flags not to ignore them because of

Week 2: Forgiveness/Acceptance

the reverence we have for God's vessels. We also have to know those in spiritual authority that we are trusting them to help navigate the spirit part of us to grow. This is why we must be led by the spirit of God when opening up spiritually because it's the essence of who we truly are.

Exercise:

Be able to be present with the feelings/emotions that you are having. I want you to journal about how you feel when this person is around. Do you find yourself doing things out of fear or obligation? Once you write, find a channel to communicate through whether that be setting a meeting or writing a letter. The purpose of the meeting or letter would be to express what you are feeling or how you have felt. Even if you do not give the letter, the letter may be able to give you the strength that you need to verbalize your thoughts.

If you have a Leader who is unwilling to acknowledge or work through what you are feeling then you have to evaluate if your season is up at this particular place. If things do not change, do not accept abuse, because you are comfortable. Do not be afraid of change!

Clause: If you have ever been hurt before by spiritual authority, take time to pray and seek God about if your season there is complete.

Week 2: Forgiveness/Acceptance

Prayer

Father in the Name of Jesus, I bind up any unforgiveness of those in authority who have done me wrong. God, I bring my heart to You, asking that You would cleanse my heart from holding oughts and offenses. God, even where there may be a root of bitterness, I ask that You would sever it, on today. Father, I ask that You would touch my mind from hurt from situations in the workplace. Heal me from a spiritual leader who has tried to intimidate me, dominate me, or control me. Lord, release me from the power of not being able to forgive. God, I come against all resistance that may be trying to form in me, to stop me from forgiving others. I release myself from all oppressive behaviors and oppressive events trying to keep me captive which happened by those in authority. God, I ask that You touch me where I may have been violated by spiritual authority. Help me to not harbor any unforgiveness towards any pastor or leader in the church. I come against any spirit that will try to hinder me from going to work (spirit of dread, the spirit of fear). Deliver me from any spirit that will try to sabotage my destiny, my spiritual walk, and prohibit me from desiring to go to church. Any spirit that causes me to say I won't trust another leader or another person who is in spiritual authority. I come against that spirit of unforgiveness that would try to make me rebel. I thank You for loosing the spirit of forgiveness, and the spirit of peace. God, I thank You for loosing the power of love and strength. God, I ask that You would set me free today. I come against every ungodly imagination and thought that would try to play over and over in my mind. I take control of my thoughts on today

Week 2: Forgiveness/Acceptance

and put on the mind of Christ. I make a choice today to forgive and through this choice, I will be set free in Jesus' Name.

Write the Thoughts of God:

_____
_____
_____
_____
_____
_____
_____
_____
_____
_____
_____
_____
_____
_____
_____
_____
_____
_____
_____
_____
_____
_____
_____

Week 2: Forgiveness/Acceptance

Write the Thoughts of God:
(Con't)

Week 2: Acceptance/Forgiveness

Saturday
Acceptance: Time To Move Forward

"Forget the former things: do not dwell on the past. See, I am doing a new thing! Now it springs up; do you not perceive it? I am making a way in the wilderness and streams in the wasteland."- Isaiah 43:18-19

It's time to receive, a mode of being receptive. We need to look at the acceptance from two perspectives: you can accept unforgiveness and hold onto. It will lead you down a negative path. On the contrary, you can accept to forgive, you will be able to move forward. A lot of people can be stuck when we don't want to accept what has happened to us and choose to not receive the truth. We don't want to receive the truth because we think it's taking away from us and not adding to us. Acceptance allows us to move forward despite all that has transpired in our lives.

Example:
If someone has dealt with a violation, they may be having a hard time accepting what has happened because the action that took place was wrong.

However, the moment this individual accepts what has taken place, they will be able to move forward vs wrestling with it. Acceptance can be challenging because it requires one to self reflect. However, the acceptance of reality brings forth healing. Once one accepts the fact that they are fearful, they are now in a position to receive faith.

Week 2: Acceptance/Forgiveness

Interaction:

Now, let's accept the past or present, and then move forward:

1. You must take an honest look at your life.
2. You should be able to identify your mistakes, if necessary.
3. You have to see what you have learned through your process.
4. You must look at the situation in order for you to move forward; instead of looking at the other party.
5. Remember to be truthful about where you are, in the process of accepting.
6. You must ask God for guidance through the healing process.
7. Lastly, you must take back your peace. Look up scriptures on peace.

For example:

Maybe you are believing God for a healing in your heart; but you are harboring unforgiveness and choosing to hold on to the pain. God requires us to forgive, but when we choose to not forgive we are walking in disobedience. Disobedience causes you to hold onto heartache, where you can't walk in the fullness of joy that God has for you. It holds you in a prison of your past or present pain. Today, we have to make a decision to choose to walk in the laws of God. We must remember forgiveness is a choice.

Week 2: Acceptance/Forgiveness

Prayer

Lord, I ask that You would help me to move forward. God, release that progression into my spirit, today. Lord, where there have been things that have come to hinder me from moving forward, release me. Things from my past, things that happened in relationships that were out of my control. Lord, deliver, and set me free from stagnation. Lord, I ask that You would touch my heart to be able to forgive; so I can be free to move forward in destiny. Also, allow me to move forward and not relive the thing that have tried to keep me captive, and hold me bound. Father, I ask that You would allow your anointing of healing and restorative power to be present even, as I pray today. Father, I am asking You to release me from guilt, from shame, from disappointment, and hurt. Father, I am asking You to empower me supernaturally to soar in Jesus' Name. Father, I thank You for breaking every stronghold in my mind, in my thoughts, in my imagination, and in my memory. I thank You that You have set me free. I believe and I receive that I have been set free. I bind up every spirit of tiredness, laziness, and fatigue. Every spirit of confusion, fear of man, fear of failing, and Father God I thank You that He who the Son sets free is free indeed. I loose the spirit of clarity, and soundness of mind. I loose faith, the wisdom of God, the courage of God, and the peace of God. I thank You for aligning me rightfully with destiny now, even as I pray this prayer, In the Mighty Name of Jesus Christ. Amen.

Week 2: Acceptance/Forgiveness

Write the Thoughts of God:

_____
_____
_____
_____
_____
_____
_____
_____
_____
_____
_____
_____
_____
_____
_____
_____
_____
_____
_____
_____
_____
_____
_____
_____

Week 2: Forgiveness/Acceptance

Write the Thoughts of God:
(Con't)

Week 3: Identification of Now

Sunday
Do You Know Who You Are?

"Consequently, you are no longer foreigners and strangers, but fellow citizens with God's people and also members of his household."-Ephesians 2:19

It is very necessary that you spend time knowing who you are, who God has divinely created you to be. It is time to know the power and the authority that is on the inside of you. Not only to understand the power, but know how to use it in the earth. An intricate part of knowing who you are, is in understanding your strengths and weaknesses. Look at areas in your life that potentially keep you stagnant. When you don't understand who God has created you to be, it causes us to leave open spaces for the enemy to come in and to move in relationships, career paths, lifestyles or experiences that God didn't intend for you to have. But when you are assured and confirmed in your God-given identity and purpose, you have to have confidence and authority. It clears a pathway in the Earth for us to fulfill purpose and destiny.

It also brings about a boldness where you will not tolerate negative things in your life. You will not allow garbage in your life. You will see yourself as a daughter of the King. When you receive and understand the confidence that comes from being a part of royalty, you walk in a form of possession for the promises of God. Anything else is too low to allow to operate in your life. Remember the queen doesn't come off her throne to deal with every situation. See yourself as an image bearer of Christ. You are image-bearer on the earth, His brand ambassador.

Week 3: Identification of Now

Exercise

Identify your strengths and your struggles and create a list. Look at the list of strengths to see how it can empower you not to struggle. How can these strengths empower you to overcome struggles? Remember it is all within you

Example:

Strength: a great organizer   *Struggle: deals with depressed/low spirits*

Strengths	Struggles
_____	_____
_____	_____
_____	_____
_____	_____
_____	_____
_____	_____
_____	_____
_____	_____

Week 3: Identification of Now

Be able to identify who God has called you to be. What is your purpose? What is your passion? You need to create boundaries and ask God to build your confidence in Him. Knowing that you can do all things through Christ has strengthened you. Let that be a declaration over yourself.

Prayer

Father in the Name of Jesus, God, I ask that you would anoint me to see myself the way You see me. God, I thank You as I walk into a new season of my life that You would build new self-worth and new self-confidence. God, I thank You that You would surround me with divine relationships and bring them into my pathway. God, I thank You that I no longer will permit let negativity, fear, doubt, skepticism, and what others think about me. Nor, will I permit past mistakes to hold me in bondage. Father, I thank You for the new freedom and authority in knowing who I am. Father, I thank You for anointing to complete every assignment in my life that You ordained. I thank You that I have the more than a conqueror anointing. Father, I thank You even as I know who I am, that You would use me to empower others. I thank You that I would no longer look at myself low or doubt myself. Father, I thank You that I will no longer walk in fear. I thank You for showing me every part of me and everything You have created about me; so that You can use it for Your glory. In Jesus' Name, Amen.

Week 3: Identification of Now

Write the Thoughts of God:

Week 3: Identification of Now

Write the Thoughts of God:
(Con't)

Week 3: Identification of Now

Monday
Why Choosing You is Important?

Scripture: I praise you because I am fearfully and wonderfully made; your works are wonderful, I know that full well.- Psalm 139:14

If you don't choose you, no one else will. You have to honor the value that God has placed on the inside of you. It is important for your mental health that you spend quality time with yourself. It may be through activities or through meditating on God's word. Also, it's important that you empower yourself by empowering positive centers of influence and circles.

I can remember a time asking my young adult daughter "Do you know who you are?" I asked her repeatedly and she even got upset with me, because she felt she was confident. What she didn't understand like many of us, knowing who you are is much more than confidence. It is walking in your God-given authority. My daughter felt the need to be responsible for someone else's thoughts or feelings, placing them as a priority before making sure her environment was healthy and whole.

You have to be aware when choosing you is important. We have to know what is healthy and unhealthy. We cannot get into a habit of pushing our feelings to the side, because that can deter us from having a healthy space and knowing when to choose us. Oftentimes, we have watched our mothers, grandmothers, aunts, or caregivers from youth to our adulthood not choose themselves and it becomes a pattern in our lives. If we continue to make decisions out of the emotional realm; and by putting

Week 3: Identification of Now

ourselves last, staying in toxic relationships, staying on jobs longer than you should, etc; it could alter your life and deter you from choosing "you". All because we have been subconsciously trained to feel bad for choosing ourselves, some may look at it as arrogance, pride, being superficial and that is not even the case.

Exercise

1} Take the time to write down and ask yourself "Why am I so available to others?"

_____

_____

_____

2} Next, get another piece of paper to introduce yourself to the world. Ask yourself "Who am I?"

3} It is more than what you like (I like yellow) and more than just being a wife, a mom, etc; but what were you created to do. What is your purpose in life?

_____

_____

_____

Week 3: Identification of Now

Prayer

Father in the Name of Jesus, I thank You right now for showing me who have created me to be. I thank You that the fire of God is making me confident and secure in who You have created me to be. I thank You that the fire of God is hitting my self-esteem, self-identity, and self-confidence. I thank You for a new knowing and surety of who I am; and that You would teach me how to walk in it every day of my life. Lord, I thank You that in times where it is tough; where I may feel that I will disappoint others or hurt others for being who you have ordained me to be; I pray that I would stand strong and choose myself. I pray that I would choose my mental stability, my emotional stability, and peace instead of people-pleasing. I pray that You would fill every void in my life and that You would continue to do a new work in me and through me. I thank You, God, that I will not despise who You have created me to be. Father, I thank You that I understand that I am fearfully and wonderfully made in Your image. Father, I thank You that You would accept the gifts and the call that You have placed upon me. God, I thank You that I would not self-sabotage. I thank You that I will walk in the fulness of the purpose of why I was created. Father, I thank You that I will begin to see myself the way You see me. Even in this change, I thank You that I will walk in a new holy boldness and confidence. Father, I thank You that You are thrusting me forward. I thank You that You have healed my heart in places where I have been disappointed, in places where I have felt pain. God, I thank You that I will hope again, and love again. I thank You, God that I will get to know who I am in

Week 3: Identification of Now

You. Father, I bind up low self-esteem, self-accusation, self-condemnation, guilt, and shame. I put on the armor of God. I thank You for mind of Christ. I thank You that the words of negativity spoken over my life, and thoughts of who others felt who I am; these words and thoughts of will not have power over my life. Even the decisions that I have made in my past, will not affect my future. I seal it with praise in Jesus' Name, I pray Amen.

Week 3: Identification of Now

Write the Thoughts of God:

Week 3: Identification of Now

Write the Thoughts of God:
(Con't)

Week 3: Identification of Now

Tuesday

Do You Have a Blueprint?

"And the Lord answered me, and said, Write the vision, and make it plain upon tables, that he may run that readeth it"- Habakkuk 2:2

It should be a priority to have a blueprint for your life. You must set goals and ask God, ask the master builder to show you the plan. This could be taking time quarterly, monthly, and yearly to see the blueprint that God has created for you and your family. When we don't have a proper blueprint to follow then we can navigate away from God's original plan and purpose for our lives. We will end up wasting time, wavering, and not being clear of our purpose in the earth. We can end up leaving out important parts out of our foundation that is necessary for God to build upon. Imagine a skyscraper at ground level, but it is missing beams to hold the weight of the building as it moves higher. Eventually, after so much weight, the structure is going to get damaged. You should acknowledge God in all things so He can direct our paths.

Exercise

Get in a quiet place and allow your mind to be still. Hear God and ask him for the blueprint for specific areas in your life:

1}Finances - _____

_____

2}Parenting - _____

_____

Week 3: Identification of Now

3} Business - _____

_____

4} Workplace - _____

_____

5} Health- _____

_____

6} Relationships - _____

_____

7} Spiritual Walk - _____

_____

Prayer

Father, I thank You for showing me the blueprint for my life. God, I ask that You would define and show me the plan You have for my life. Father, You said in Your word that if I would acknowledge You in all of my ways that You would direct my path. God, I thank You for directing my path in this new season of my life. Father, I thank You for making it plain to me what You have orchestrated and ordained in my life. God, I thank You for giving me prophetic insight to be able to see; and for You to navigate me through the plans that You have created for my life. Father, I thank You for every plan and I agree with what You are doing and going to do in my life. God, I thank You that You will bring it to pass. I thank You for Your grace and mercy as I walk out this blueprint. I ask that you would make every crooked way straight. I pray that You would give me peace in my thoughts and peace throughout this journey. God, as I follow You I know that the promises shall come to past, in Jesus' Name, Amen.

Week 3: Identification of Now

Write the Thoughts of God:

Week 3: Identification of Now

Write the Thoughts of God:
(Con't)

Week 3: Identification of Now

Wednesday
Operational Plan

For which of you, intending to build a tower, sitteth not down first, and counters the cost, whether he have sufficient to finish it? -14:28

Do you desire to achieve financial freedom? Oftentimes, people desire to achieve financial freedom. Then put a plan in place to achieve this goal, however, they struggle to reach their final destination. The first step in following a plan to get to your destination is to know where you are currently located. This is a very important step, here is an operational plan to help you navigate throughout this journey.

The purpose of this operational plan is to help you identify where you are currently located financially. Take a moment to honestly fill out the form below with all of your expenses and all of your income sources then complete this operational plan:

After completing your operational plan, identify if you have an overflow or a shortage of income.

If you have an overflow then look at options of investing and/or saving.

If you have a shortage then you have two options:

1) Cut your expenses.

2) Increase your income.

Week 3: Identification of Now

Genesis Wealth Management Operational Plan: 313-733-7374

MONTHLY INCOME		MONTHLY EXPENSES	
Item	Amount/Month	Item	Amount/Month
After Tax Wages	$	Rent/Mortgage	$
Tips or Bonuses	$	Utilities (electric, heat)	$
Child Support	$	Utilities (water)	$
Alimony	$	Food (groceries)	$
DHHS FIP (Cash Assistance)	$	Food (restaurants)	$
Social Security	$	Telephone and cell phone	$
SSI	$	Internet/Cable	$
Retirement/Pension	$	Transportation (car payment)	$
Unemployment	$	Transportation (gas, bus fare)	$
Veterans Benefits	$	Tuition and other education fees	$
Bridge Card (food stamps)	$	Student loans	$
Other	$	Credit Cards	$
		Insurance (health, car)	$
		Child care	$
Total Monthly Income	$	Child support	$
Total Monthly Expenses	$	Personal (toiletries, clothing)	$
Budget Surplus/Deficit	$	Other	$

Declare This Statement Aloud:

I read the above budget and I commit to using it to help pay my bills one time Father I honor You, I glorify You. I bless Your name.

Now that you have completed the form you are on your way to financial freedom.

In summary, here are three basic steps to assist you:

1. Identify where you are currently located (Complete the operational plan).

2. Identify where you want to go (Set goals).

3. Create a plan of action (What are you going to commit to?)

By: Dr. Wes Warren

Week 3: Identification of Now

Prayer

Father, I come to You in repentance for a lack of organization in my finances. Lord, I ask that you would breathe pneuma onto my financial system and structure. God, I thank You for the fire in the finances. Lord, I ask that You would increase what You have given me. Lord, I thank You for new ideas and inventions, even new business plans. I thank You that I will not fear. I bind up all lack, shortage, and insufficiency in the Name of Jesus. I loose the spirit of increase and prosperity to be upon my finances. I thank You as I give; it shall be given unto me, good measure, press down, shaken together, and runneth over shall men give unto my bosom. I thank Lord, God for what You are doing in my financial system. God, I thank you that I will be obedient to the operational plan that You have given me for my household. God, I ask that You would show me where there is frivolous spending and where there is no structure in the spending. God, I thank You that You will show me new ways to save money and new ways to bring in revenue. I bind up insufficient funds, late payments, and shut off notices in the Name of Jesus. God, I thank You that there would be order in the finances and I thank You for increasing what you already have given me, in the Name of Jesus Christ. Amen

Week 3: Identification of Now

Write the Thoughts of God:

Week 3: Identification of Now

Write the Thoughts of God:
(Con't)

Week 3: Identification of Now

Thursday
The Power of the Atmosphere that You Carry

In the beginning, God created the heavens and the earth. 2 Now the earth was formless and empty, darkness was over the surface of the deep, and the Spirit of God was hovering over the waters. And God said, "Let there be light," and there was light.-Genesis 1:1-3

You are the atmosphere you carry. You are an atmosphere within a larger atmosphere. You have a personal atmosphere wherever you go; keep it clear, conducive, and positive. No more time for negativity, toxicity, doubt. The atmosphere that you carry will gravitate to whatever it is giving. Your atmosphere has to be conducive for others, to connect with those who are exuberant. Ultimately, to push you forward. Do the work to maintain a healthy atmosphere as possible. Begin to build antibodies against negativity, to repel it. Do not tolerate that in your atmosphere; it brings a disconnect. You want to be able to have healthy thought patterns, healthy habits, and behaviors, or lifestyle. You will be able to have a clear mind and focus. What you are bringing into the atmosphere is what the earth will yield to you.

Exercise

What is your atmosphere saying to you? Discern what your atmosphere is speaking to you. Write down what you hear or what you feel? If it's an atmosphere that is unhealthy begin to declare the word of God. If you feel that your atmosphere is good and healthy ask God to bring more love, joy, peace in your atmosphere.

Week 3: Identification of Now

Prayer

Father, I thank You for an atmosphere that is conducive for miracles, signs, and wonders to flow in my life. God, I thank You that if there is anything negative or unhealthy in my personal atmosphere, in my thoughts, in my home, in my car, or in my workplace, I ask that You would remove it now. God, thank You for giving me the fruit of the Spirit, that I may be able to function in them. God, thank You for even giving me patience with others and with myself. God, I thank You for releasing new angels in my atmosphere and new joy. Lord, I thank You for anointing my ear-gates to hear and receive joy and glad tidings. Lord, I thank You that You would assign joy to my ear gates and kind words to my lips. God, I thank You that even if I see the negative, I would decree and declare the positive outcome in my atmosphere. God, I thank You for causing me to be an environmental change agent. God, I thank You that as I walk into atmospheres, that I can change atmospheres because I have been in Your presence. God, I ask that You would allow Your glory to rest in my personal atmosphere, wherever I may go. Father, I thank You for the peace of God, the strength of God, the love of God, and the joy of God being upon me now, that everywhere I go You would be with me, in Jesus' Name, Amen.

Week 3: Identification of Now

Write the Thoughts of God:

Week 3: Identification of Now

Write the Thoughts of God:
(Con't)

Week 3: Identification of Now

Friday
Beauty From the Inside Out

She is clothed with strength and dignity, and she laughs without fear of the future.- Proverbs 31:25

What does it mean to be beautiful? The world is superficial. I am a believer that beauty begins from within. Oftentimes, we beautify ourselves outwardly; but really, we are disappointed, hurting, neglected, violated, afraid, and ashamed. As women, we have mastered nails, hair, outfits, makeup to be flawless but we are married on the inside. It is imperative that we pamper our spirits, that we take time to cultivate our relationship with God. Because our spiritual side is really who we are not just how we appear to the natural eye. We have to allow the beauty from within to radiate through us which means we can't carry old baggage. We have to learn how to forgive, repent, and do internal plastic surgery. Just like we have appointments to assure we are beautified on the outside, we have to keep them with Abba to maintain the beauty from within.

Week 3: Identification of Now

Exercise

Take time to write down any lie that the enemy has told you about who you are then denounce it. Then decree and declare in the world who God says you are even if you don't see it!

Lies:_____
_____
_____
_____
_____
_____
_____
_____
_____

Truth:_____
_____
_____
_____
_____
_____
_____
_____

Week 3: Identification of Now

Prayer

Father, I thank You and praise You! Lord, I ask where I have been hurt and rejected, that You would begin to let me see myself the way You see me. I thank You, God for going into my heart, my mind, my soul, and heal me where I am broken and disappointed. I thank You, God, as I read this book that I would transform, be set free, and delivered. I thank You that I will know that I am precious, valuable, and worthy of love. I thank You that I will walk in who You mandated me to be. I thank You that my feet are bound to Your will for my life. I thank You that I will know that I am beautiful. I thank You that I will know in my story, the trials, and tribulations of what I have been through; that You are the great orchestrator and the Author & Finisher of my Faith. I thank You for giving me a crown to wear to be a Queen on the Earth. My prayer is that God, You would allow me to see the real me: for I am fearfully and wonderfully made. I pray that I will carry new fragrances and new aroma that only comes from spending time with the King. Lord, adorn me a new crown: give me beauty for ashes. I will no longer identify myself by what man thinks or what I may have thought; but identified myself as the Daughter of the King. I bind up low self-esteem, low self-worth, lack of value towards myself, comparing myself to others. I bind negative thoughts towards my body, self-image, lack of self-care, lack of confidence. I release in my heart and mind the confidence of God. I put on the strength of God and walk in the authority of Christ. I put on my breastplate of righteousness and cover my mind with the helmet of salvation. I release the anointing of Esther to be upon me, the boldness

Week 3: Identification of Now

of Deborah to upon me, and the anointing of the inner strength from Ruth. I count it done. I am a new creation in Jesus' Name. Amen.

Write the Thoughts of God:

Week 3: Identification of Now

Write the Thoughts of God:
(Con't)

Week 3: Identification of Now

Saturday

Staying Heart Happy

"A joyful heart is good medicine but a crushed spirit dries up the bones." - Proverbs 17:22

Don't allow the spirit of jealousy, disappointment, envy, and anger in your heart. Keep your heart happy and happy heart towards others. Maintaining love is the standard attitude. We have to check our hearts when we feel the enemy trying to create yokes or frustration within us. Ask God to purge our hearts from all unrighteousness. Did you know out of the heart flows the issues of life? As God cleanses our hearts, we have to guard our hearts. We need to love man out of hearts and God with all our hearts. As people we disappoint but God does not. If there is any awkwardness in your heart, you have to check it and make sure you get rid of anything that is contrary to being heart happy.

Exercise

1} Answer the following questions to help you identify your season now.

2} Are you happy with your life now? When was the last time you took a vacation? Do you feel accomplished? How are your finances?

3} Here are some things to get you on track
   a. What makes you happy?
   b. What are some goals you want to accomplish?
   c. Where are some places you want to travel?

Week 3: Identification of Now

    d. Keeping a positive attitude.

    e. Seeing yourself through the eyes of God.

    f. "Loving you Beauty from the Inside Out".

Prayer

Father, I thank You for a happy heart. Father, I ask that You would give me a heart of flesh. I bind up every stoney heart, every evil heart, every black heart, every wicked heart, every angry heart, every offensive heart, every rejected heart, every disappointed heart, every despondent heart, every disgruntled heart, every aching heart, every bleeding heart, I come against. I pray that You would bring healing to every area of the heart. God, even where there are long-standing issues, where there are matters of the heart, go in and touch with Your nail-scarred hand and bring healing in the heart. Lord, heal my heart from heartache and heart pain. God, I thank You for filling any leak or hole in my heart. Lord, heal me and deliver me from the wounded heart, the traumatized heart, the unstable heart, the deceptive heart, the lying heart. God, give me a heart of flesh, a heart that is flexible and pliable. Father, I thank You for teaching me how to guard my heart, because out of it flows the issues of life. God, I thank You for touching my emotional state. Help me to have a paradigm shift in my mind and my thinking. God, I thank You for loosing the heart of contempt, the heart of peace, the heart of joy, the heart of meekness, the heart of kindness, the heart of long-suffering, the heart of diligence, the heart of the agape love, the heart of the Father. God, I thank You for loosing your agape love to flow through my heart, that I would operate in a new mantle and measure of Your love.

Week 3: Identification of Now

Write the Thoughts of God:

Week 3: Identification of Now

Write the Thoughts of God:
(Con't)

Week 4: Fulfillment The Mindset of Champion

Sunday
What Are You Thinking?

"Finally, brothers and sisters, whatever is true, whatever is noble, whatever is right, whatever is pure, whatever is lovely, whatever is admirable—if anything is excellent or praiseworthy—think about such things."-Philippians 4:8

Do you sometimes get overwhelmed, as if you cannot move forward? No matter how hard you try, it seems as if you are in a stage of stagnation; spiritually or naturally? Sometimes in our lives, we begin our journey without all the avenues it entails. We didn't understand that we had to conquer our fears and uncertainties. In some cases, we were fighting against something much greater; those unseen forces that have been passed down from generation to generation (this would be considered a generational curse) My hope and prayer would be for you to recognize what you think about daily.

Exercise
Take today if you have time at home as thoughts come in your mind begin to write them down… thoughts concerning you or thoughts connected to others.

_____
_____
_____
_____
_____

Week 4: Fulfillment The Mindset of Champion

If you are driving today, do not turn on the radio. Instead, listen to what you are thinking. Write these thoughts down (once you stop driving). Look at what you wrote and listen to what you have been thinking!

_____
_____
_____
_____
_____
_____
_____
_____
_____
_____
_____
_____
_____
_____

Prayer

Father in the Name of Jesus, God, I repent for negative thoughts concerning myself. God, I ask You would anoint me to see myself the way You see me. I am fearfully and wonderfully made. God, I am asking where I have thoughts that are negative that you would change the paradigm in my thinking. Help me, to have healthy thoughts towards myself and others. Teach me, how to keep my mind, and thoughts healthy; and keep my emotions stable in Jesus' Name. Father, I know the thoughts that You have towards me are good and not evil. Father, teach me how to focus on what is true and honest. Father, I bind up every lie

Week 4: Fulfillment The Mindset of Champion

Prayer: con't
that the enemy may bring concerning my life, concerning my situation, and even others around me. Lord, teach me not to assume and to think negatively, first; concerning situations that may not go as I had planned. Lord, wash my thoughts on today and wash my mind on today. I dismantle every stronghold of negative thinking, God, go into every neurological pathway; where I have experienced trauma, drama, and pain. God, allow the oil of joy to flow through my mind. Father, I thank You for new neurological pathways being created through positive thinking and healthy experiences. Lord, allow me to see the great things You are doing in my life and not focus n what I feel is going wrong. Teach me, not to compare myself, my situation, or my life to others but to walk in the fullness of who You have created me to be. Hallelujah and Amen, in the Jesus' Name.

Affirmations
I am healed in my spirit, soul, and body.
I choose to believe God.
I am more than a conqueror.
I can do all things through Christ who gives me strength.
I am joint-heirs with Christ Jesus seated in heavenly places.
I am the daughter of a King.
I shall fulfill my purpose.
Give and it shall be given.
I am fearfully and wonderfully made.
I don't lose I learn.
I find beauty in being me.

Week 4: Fulfillment The Mindset of A Champion

Write the Thoughts of God:

Week 4: Fulfillment The Mindset of A Champion

Write the Thoughts of God:
(Con't)

Week 4: Fulfillment The Mindset of A Champion

Monday

What's in Your Soil?

And be not conformed to this world: but be ye transformed by the renewing of your mind, that ye may prove what is that good, and acceptable, and perfect, will of God.- Romans 12:2

The type of soil you have is important because it fertilizes seeds. We need to learn to protect our soil. Did you know that certain seeds cannot grow in certain types of soil? We must look at the seeds that are in our soil. What is the inside of the mind? Is it rejection, loneliness, low self-esteem or other negative thoughts? For example, one may have to get rid of thoughts of rejection so that when those seeds come around, then thoughts of rejection won't germinate. We need to check to see if our soil is healthy. We want the negative seeds to be rejected and positive seeds to be able to germinated. We must examine the soil to see if it is suitable for planting. Sometimes debris can get in the soil: <u>glass</u>, <u>trash</u>, <u>rocks</u>, <u>weeds</u>, and <u>clay</u>. Look to see if your soil (your mind) can fertilize the seeds that have been planted.

Exercise:

Yesterday you took the time to look at your thoughts. Now it's time to look at the root system of the thoughts (soil)... what is growing? Why are you thinking about what you are thinking? _____
_____
_____
_____

Week 4: Fulfillment The Mindset of A Champion

Prayer:

Father, I thank You for purging my soil. God, I ask that You would bring deliverance to places I have been hurt, rejected, and disappointed. God, I ask that You would heal my heart. Father, I thank You that my thoughts would be stable concerning my life. Thank you for emotional stability. Father, I ask that my soil would have the right ingredients for positive seeds to grow. Lord, I thank You that my thoughts would align with Your thoughts towards myself and others. God, I thank You that I will think about the things that are true. Even when the enemy tries to present things that are lies, that the soul in my thoughts would not be a place where they can grow. God, I thank You for divine thoughts, thoughts that are God-centered. Father, I thank You for thoughts that are inspired by You. Thank You for your creative thoughts. Father, I thank You I will no longer live in an unbalanced state in my emotions. God, I thank you that you are breaking up those hard places. God, I thank You for allowing new rivers to flow. God, I thank You that I will no longer be stuck in my past; but I will press forward into my future. Father, I thank You that I would be able to receive hope, love, and soundness of mind today. God, I thank You that I receive healing today! We count it done, in Jesus' Name.

Week 4: Fulfillment The Mindset of A Champion

Write the Thoughts of God:

Week 4: Fulfillment The Mindset of A Champion

Write the Thoughts of God:
(Con't)

_____
_____
_____
_____
_____
_____
_____
_____
_____
_____
_____
_____
_____
_____
_____
_____
_____
_____
_____
_____
_____
_____
_____
_____

Week 4: Fulfillment The Mindset of A Champion

Tuesday
An Interview with My Thoughts

Let this mind be in you, which was also in Christ Jesus:- Philippians 2:5

It is crucial that we take the time to interview our thoughts. You may wonder, what is interviewing my thoughts? After we take the time to hear what we are thinking, it is time we get to the root of what we are thinking. Then we can examine if these thoughts fit with the life God has for us. We must watch our thoughts, because they become active; they can be used in actions consciously or subconsciously. Our thoughts can create a false reality of fear, insecurity, and negativity.

Exercise:

Just like any interview: It is time to have an interview with your own thoughts.

Take the time to sit down and look at your thoughts from yesterday and ask yourself; "Do these thoughts fit? "Am I going to act out these thoughts and let them manifest into my life?"

Finally, decide if these thoughts are okay. Is that what I truly want in my life?

Remember we are human, we are subject to have thoughts, and some are going to be contrary to the will of God. We have to know and learn to keep the thoughts into the obedience of Christ (For the weapons of our warfare are not carnal, but mighty through God to the pulling down of strongholds, II Corinthians 10:4).

Week 4: Fulfillment The Mindset of A Champion

Prayer:

Father, I ask that You would forgive me forgive me for any sin, any thought, action or deed that was contrary to Your will. Father, I thank You because on this day You are renewing my thoughts and renewing my mind. For You said in Your word, that I would have this mind amongst myself which is Yours in Christ Jesus. Father, I thank You right now that my mind is thinking on those things that are just and those things that are of a good report. Father, destroy every lofty opinion raised against the knowledge of God and I take into captivity every thought that is not of You. I thank You that the joy of the Lord will be my strength. I bind up the spirit of fear; fear of being alone, fear of looking through my thoughts, fear of what I think of myself, fear of what people have said against me, and all doors that may have been opened up. God, I thank You right now that every demonic portal that will try to come and attack my mind is sealed now. I thank You right now that I am aligning myself with what Heaven has to say concerning me and what God's will and agenda is for my life. Therefore, if anyone is in Christ, the new creation has come. The old has gone, the new is here (II Corinthians 5:17). I promise to give You the praise in Jesus' Name. Amen.

Week 4: Fulfillment The Mindset of A Champion

Write the Thoughts of God:

Week 4: Fulfillment The Mindset of A Champion

Write the Thoughts of God:
(Con't)

Week 4: Fulfillment The Mindset of A Champion

Wednesday
Identifying Emotional Distress

When my anxious inner thoughts become overwhelming, your comfort encourages me. -Psalm 94:19

Do you ever find yourself in seasons where your emotions are all over the place? You really can't complete thoughts? Do you really understand the actions that you are abstaining from? It's important if you enter a season like this that you take the time to see where the emotional distress is coming from. Have you ever been in a place where spiritually it seems like you are not at rest or at peace? Have you ever felt like your emotions are not matching the manifestation of what you are producing naturally?

Example: It can look like someone is happy and things are in order but emotionally this person is not balanced. They are depressed or sad on the inside.

When you find that you are in cycle or season when this is happening, you need to create time to identify emotionally where you are. So that way, God can bring peace in the realm of your emotions. It is the plot of the enemy to have us live life, to be present naturally and absent emotionally or even spiritually.

Week 4: Fulfillment The Mindset of A Champion

Exercise:

Take some time to identify areas or seasons in your life; triggers, people, places that may cause you to go into emotional distress.

Write down what disrupts the peace and harmony of your spirit.

_____
_____
_____
_____
_____
_____
_____
_____
_____
_____

Example: Being around environments of yelling and hostility, not completing assignments, or feeling like you aren't living up to personal goals.

Next, identify and separate your emotion from what's factual. When these things happen (different triggers or situations) you need to be able not to act out of your emotions. However, you need to take ownership of the emotion and making sure they are manifesting in your life with peace and harmony.

Week 4: Fulfillment The Mindset of A Champion

Example: You could be angry or depressed.
How do I bring peace and harmony to my emotions?
   1) Get counseling.
   2) Decide to dismiss yourself from the situation.
   3) Participate in an activity you enjoy

Are you manifesting the chaos of what you are thinking? It starts in the mind. You need to be at peace so you do not miss the moment. Let the manifestations of your motivation match. Your actions need to align with what you are saying. Taking the time to be at peace will cause stability emotionally.

Prayer:
Dear Lord Jesus, I thank You for taking control of my emotions. Lord, I surrender my anxiety, my fears, my discomforts, my distrust, my disappointments, my anger and I give it to You. I ask that You would intervene in the emotional realm of my inner thinking. I thank You for bringing peace and that You would bring balance. Father, I know that if I trust in You, You would show me the path in which You ordained for my life. God, I ask that even in times of uncertainty and anger and times of anxiety and disappointment, that You show me how to react. I thank You, Father, that I would not act out of distress. Also, to help me not make decisions out of distress. Father, I thank You for teaching me how to allow peace to be still in my thoughts so that I can hear from You. I thank You for giving me direction and guidance in the moments that I am being affected emotionally by the things that are going on. Father, I

Week 4: Fulfillment The Mindset of A Champion

thank You for the Peace of God, that surpasses all natural understanding. I thank You for bringing healing and deliverance in my emotions in Jesus' Name. Amen

Write the Thoughts of God:

_____
_____
_____
_____
_____
_____
_____
_____
_____
_____
_____
_____
_____
_____
_____
_____

Week 4: Fulfillment The Mindset of A Champion

Write the Thoughts of God:
(Con't)

Week 4: Fulfillment The Mindset of Champion

Thursday
The Power of Focus

"No, dear brothers and sisters, I have not achieved it, but I focus on this one thing: Forgetting the past and looking forward to what lies ahead,"- Philippians 3:13

Focus is the state or quality of having or producing clear definition. The power of focus is vital to manifesting a champion mindset. Often times, we are easily distracted by life experiences. When one builds a healthy mind, it produces healthy thoughts and ultimately produces healthy actions. When you can focus on the vision God has given you, it produces self-confidence. It also gives you a peace that comes from within; in knowing, that you are clear in what God has called you to manifest in the Earth. When we focus, you put yourself in a position to be more mindful of what we feel; to be actually present in moments that are occurring in your life.

As humans, we have to learn to be determined to gain focus in every area of our lives. Discipline plays a great part in manifesting the powerful tool of focus. When you do not allow the power of focus in manifesting, you can be easily distracted from fulfilling our God-given destiny. This is why we must maintain focus, no matter what. You must practice and exercise discipline, daily. Starting through small tasks, because ultimately it provides the power of focus. How well your focus is can determine the volume of positive outcomes that you produce in your life. When you begin to focus on things that you want to accomplish, you will discover that you will see more positive outcomes.

Week 4: Fulfillment The Mindset of Champion

Exercise:

Take some time to focus on some things that you know your spirit has been leading you to do and some desires you would like to accomplish as it aligns with God's purpose for your life.

The word of God tells us to write the vision and make it plan (Habakkuk 2:2). Take the time to write your vision board and begin to allow the discipline of focus to manifest what God has promised you. Write a list of the things that you are believing God for, and be intentional about your actions and moving in the direction of what you are believing will happen in your life. See it, believe it, and achieve it.

_____

_____

_____

_____

_____

_____

_____

_____

_____

_____

_____

_____

Week 4: Fulfillment The Mindset of Champion

Prayer:

I call on the Omnipotent and Sovereign God. The Holy One who gives me the power to not be divided away from Him, from His love, His protection, and His guidance. Father, I thank You that Your word says You would lead and guide me into all truth, when I trust You. I thank You for the power to focus and I thank You giving me the discipline to see things through your vision, that You have orchestrated and designed for my life. I pray that I will not miss anything that You have promised me. God, I thank You right now for empowering me to focus. I thank You for moving out distractions and moving out things that will hinder me and detour me away from completing the tasks that you have orchestrated for me. Lord, I surrender my will, my mind, and my heart to you. I ask that You would endow me with a supernatural ability to focus, to keep my eyes fixed on You no matter what life may bring my way. In Jesus' Name, Amen.

Week 4: Fulfillment The Mindset of Champion

Write the Thoughts of God:

_____
_____
_____
_____
_____
_____
_____
_____
_____
_____
_____
_____
_____
_____
_____
_____
_____
_____
_____
_____
_____
_____
_____
_____
_____
_____

Week 4: Fulfillment The Mindset of A Champion

Write the Thoughts of God:
(Con't)

Week 4: Fulfillment The Mindset of Champion

Friday
Pushing Forward

"No, dear brothers and sisters, I have not achieved it, but I focus on this one thing: Forgetting the past and looking forward to what lies ahead,"- Philippians 3:13

It's nothing more important than the final push. When we push we see things manifest. There is a point in our lives that we are going to have to push. We are going to have to push past obstacles, push past resistance, push past uncertainties, push past barriers, and push past generational curses. We have to push, we cannot give up!

Now that you have reached this portion of the journal, you are at the point of pushing. You are at the climax of a paradigm shift in your mind. God will have you begin to reflect and go over some of the things that you wrote down in this journal. Even going back over some emotions that were brought up, some of the things God showed you, some of the promises that he told you. Now the pieces of the puzzle will begin to come together where you need to push. You have to begin to push, you have to know that you are not weak, but you are strong and courageous.

Sometimes when you push, you are going to feel resistance, you are going to feel a push back, but don't let that stop you. You must take hold of the things we have talked about; focus, faith, peace, tilling your soil, interviewing your thoughts. Now, do not let the resistance that would try to push back, as you push forward, stop you from moving in the place mentally and emotionally where God has called you to be.

Week 4: Fulfillment The Mindset of Champion

Exercise:

1) I want you to write down three things that you are believing God for in the next 90 days. These three things need to seem out of reach but something you know you would have to push past resistance in order to obtain.

    a)

    b)

    c)

2) Look at areas in your life where you feel it has been a push back. I want you to use some of the techniques and some of the things that you wrote and read about over this month to fight the resistance.

I want you to see yourself pushing forward. See yourself pushing the agenda that God has for your life and pushing it forward. I want you to see it.

Yesterday, we talked about doing the vision board. Seeing it, believing it, and achieving it. Now, I want you to examine these specific areas that there has been resistance, I want you to push it forward. Whether you have experienced resistance of depression or oppression, the resistance of starting your business, the resistance of your heart being disappointed, or traumatized. I want you to see it pushing forward and begin to exercise and walk in it as if it was not in your way. It takes work.

Week 4: Fulfillment The Mindset of Champion

Example: If your resistance is in starting your business, start by getting a name for the business. Then getting it registered, writing the vision, and more. Whatever it is, there needs to be a pushing forward that takes place.

Prayer: The Prophetic Push
Father in the Name of Jesus, I thank You for the prophetic push. I thank You for the wind that pushes me forward. God, I thank You that I will not go back from what You have delivered me from. I pray that I will move forward in what You called me to. I thank You, Lord, that I am becoming who you have ordained for me to be. Father, I thank You for strengthening my mind, strengthening my heart, and strengthening my relationship with You. God, I thank You for giving me inner peace and that my paradigm in my mind and in my thinking will shift. I thank You that I will move forward. I thank You that I will not get forget the former, but press forward to the mark and the high call which is in Christ Jesus. Lord, I thank You right now that I will not get stuck or complacent. Lord, I thank You that even as the enemy tries to push back or cause resisters in my life, I thank You that it will break by the power of the Holy Ghost. Lord, I thank You that I am not in the same place as I started on this journey. I thank You lord, that there has been a paradigm shift in my thinking. I thank You that I will not go back, look back or talk back but I would move expeditiously forward in You in Jesus' Name. Amen.

Week 4: Fulfillment The Mindset of A Champion

Write the Thoughts of God:

Week 4: Fulfillment The Mindset of A Champion

Write the Thoughts of God:
(Con't)

Week 4: Fulfillment The Mindset of Champion

Saturday

The Mindset of a Champion

"No, dear brothers and sisters, I have not achieved it, but I focus on this one thing: Forgetting the past and looking forward to what lies ahead,"- Philippians 3:13

We have arrived. This has been a beautiful journey for those who have completed this journal. Some will not complete it; but for those of you who have, it is my prayer, it is my hope, it is my desire, and God's desire, that a shift has taken place. A shift in your mind and your emotions. A shift that has taken place in the depths of who you are to call you present, to call you forward, and to call you healed. Also, to call you into a place from this day forward, to do the work necessary regarding yourself and your spirit. You have been given the tools to keep your spirit clear, your thoughts disciplined to remain focused, aware of the times and seasons in your life, and to awaken you where God has called you to go.

A mindset of a champion is a mind that does not allow defeat to keep them bound in what they felt may have defeated/discouraged them. Instead, this mind learns from areas of challenges, resistance, or disappointment. It creates a stepping stone to trailblazer new paths in your life and the life of others.

During this journey of self-reflection, I hope that you will take the time to look back over where you have started. Use this as an opportunity to see if you have grown any from your past and present. Have you had the chance to use any of the techniques in new challenges as you were

Week 4: Fulfillment The Mindset of Champion

completing the journal? Did you grow?

It is my hope, it is my sincere desire that there has been some growth. If there has been any growth, you need to celebrate this victory. Be happy about it, be present during the moment.

For some of you, this may be the first time you finished a workbook. Celebrate it, celebrate the completion by doing self-care. You took the time to care about your mind, now you are in a new place of awareness of your thoughts, emotions ,and who you are. Do not be afraid to walk in the new you. Do not be afraid to express your feelings or desires. Do not keep things bottle up on the inside, where it begins to eat away at you mentally or even physically.

Thank you for being vulnerable and honest. Thank you for doing the work. Continue to be still and know that He is God.

Week 4: Fulfillment The Mindset of Champion

Activity: CELEBRATE THE COMPLETION OF TAKING TIME TO WORK ON YOU!

Example: Go buy yourself your favorite food, eat a cupcake, go shopping, etc in someway celebrate what you have accomplished.

Although, you may not see a lot of natural manifestations; just yet, just know that what is done in the Spirit cannot be reversed, changed, or altered in the natural!

Week 4: Fulfillment The Mindset of Champion

Write the Thoughts of God:

Week 4: Fulfillment The Mindset of A Champion

Write the Thoughts of God:
(Con't)

CONTACT PAGE

Facebook: Woman 2 Woman Int'l

Instagram: @Woman2Womanintl

Website: www.Woman2Womanintl.com

Email: woman2womangenesis@gmail.com

Phone number: 734-680-8369